Confidence In 24 Hours

Step Into Your Power

By Ania Jeffries. Award Winning Coach, Confidence Generator, No 1 International Best Selling Coauthor, Radio Broadcaster, Founder Women Work, Mentor Princes Trust

MTNMedia

CONTENTS

FOREWORD

You are witnessing a new generation growing up in an era of smart phones and social media. You expect immediate responses to texts, emails, and calls, and unless this response is instant, moments of self-doubt, low self-belief and lack of confidence can potentially kick in.

However, this new digital world offers a wonderful platform for you to confidently express yourself creatively and independently. It also offers a space for you to discuss how you look and feel about your physical, emotional and mental health. High confidence and self-esteem is key to positive mental health, so finding a toolkit such as *Confidence in 24 Hours,* that can support you at any age, at any time of your life, to grow in confidence and self-belief across different areas of your personal and business life, is of huge value.

Ania Jeffries is an award-winning coach, an international bestselling coauthor, and a highly sought-after resource for personal growth, transformation and self-development. She has chosen to write this book in order to give you the necessary tools to be confident, to live your life with purpose, and to create a life of happiness and value. She is a real live wire who breezes into any room with a smile as wide as a mile, whirls around like a hurricane, and is passionate about creating positive change in your life. Her mission is to empower you to inspire the next generation to unleash their full potential, to become confident and unstoppable in achieving your dreams.

This book is the first step to support you to take control of and make positive changes in your life.

Raymond Aaron
New York Times Bestselling Author

ACKNOWLEDGEMENTS

This book is dedicated to my wonderful family; to my gorgeous husband, Simon; my beautiful children, Anousha, Mimi, and Ben; and also to my twin, Basia, and brothers George and Richard. Thank you for always believing in me and supporting me to not only live my dreams but to Dream, Think, and Play Big. As Les Brown always says, "Shoot for the moon, and if you miss, you'll be among the stars." Each and every one of you inspire me every day, more than you realise, to have the courage to know that everything is possible. And it so is!

This book is my gift to you.

My vision

"My vision is to build the global platform for entrepreneurs to connect, communicate and collaborate with confidence."

Ania Jeffries

CHAPTER 1:

HOW TO CREATE A POSITIVE MINDSET

"What consumes your mind, controls your life." – **Unknown**

Mindset is all about attitude—how you approach the world and deal with your experiences each day—whether you approach life with a positive attitude and a big, fat smile, or whether you approach life with a negative attitude: constantly criticising yourself and judging others; looking for things to go wrong or to fail; allowing the negative inner voice, the devil that sits on your shoulder, to whisper to you, to kick in, limit, and control you.

STEPS TO CREATE A POSITIVE MINDSET

1. You have a choice as to how you create your mindset, from the moment you wake up. What is the first thought that pops into your mind when you wake up? Is it positive or negative? Do you allow that thought to set the tone for the rest of the day? Do you reframe it? Does it serve you? How does it serve you?

2. Start the day with a positive affirmation. Positive affirmations are used to reprogram your thought patterns and change the way you think and feel about things. Find an affirmation that works for you. Dr Google is great. So, whenever you are in need of positivity, repeat a positive affirmation to yourself. Here are a couple of examples that are great to start with: "All is well;" "I have enough."

3. Find humour in bad situations. Every time you find some humour in a difficult situation, you win. How many times have you been in a situation where it has been difficult to see any positive in your situation, and someone has cracked a joke that made you laugh. A well-timed one-liner can turn a tense moment into a lighter one, and the mood will change, even if just for a minute. Laughing not only benefits you but everyone around you, and those who laugh more live longer and happier lives.

4. Transform negative self-talk into positive self-talk. The first step is to recognise your own negative self-talk. So, start to raise awareness of it. Write down how many times a day you allow a negative thought to pop into your head. Reflect on the direction this self-talk takes you in. If you say to yourself that you are ugly, or beautiful, you are probably right either way because the words you use with yourself will eventually become your reality. What words do you use with yourself every day? Think of your mind as a computer. Press return to continue the conversation, or delete, to put the thought into the trash can. Positive thinkers are aware of this self-talk and are able to block or reframe, to reverse the language.

5. Surround yourself with positive people. You become 5 of the people you most hang around with, so reflect on whether your biggest influencers are of a positive or a negative influence. The more you surround yourself with toxic people, the bigger your negative mindset. It's contagious. Walk away from the moaners; set some boundaries. Look to solely surround yourself with individuals who are happy and positive, and inspire you to achieve greater goals. Your life will flourish and become brighter, not only for yourself but also for your family, your friends, your work, and your community.

6. Turn failures into successes: There is always a positive lesson in every failure. Rather than beating yourself up about what you haven't achieved, why don't you focus on all that you have achieved, and on the positive lessons you have learnt from this situation, not only about yourself but about others. Write them down and then praise/reward yourself. Acknowledge you have stepped out of your comfort zone; it wasn't easy, but you did it! You took action and moved to the next level of personal growth. You should stand tall and feel very proud.

7. Focus on the present: I want you to focus—not on today, not on this morning, not on this afternoon, not on the next few hours— I want you to focus on the *now*. Ask yourself if what is happening is as bad as you think it is. Most negative thoughts stem from a memory. We tend to exaggerate an event or a situation through our imagination. So, stay in the present moment.

HOW TO CREATE A POSITIVE MINDSET:

EXERCISE 1:

Affirmations (or statements) are a wonderful way to create positive thinking, greater productivity, and self- empowerment. They can challenge and help overcome self-sabotaging and negative thoughts. Repeat them several times a day, with feeling, as soon as a negative thought or behaviour kicks in. Negative thoughts can become self-fulfilling prophecies; so, when you start to counter them with positive affirmations, you drive positive change in your career, in yourself, in your business, and in your home life. They work really well alongside visualisation; so, in addition to picturing the change you would like to see, write it down and say it aloud.

Think about the areas of your life that you would like to change. Write down several behaviours or areas that you would like to focus on. Be sure they are aligned with your core values so you feel genuinely inspired to action them. And ensure they are realistic. Always write them down in the present tense. For example, if you are worried about a new project in the office, say to yourself, "This project IS going to be incredible." Other examples of affirmations:

- I AM whole and awesome just as I am.

- I AM radiating with love and compassion.

- I AM successful in every which way.

- I CAN do this on my own.

- My team respect and value my opinion.

- I AM overflowing with abundance.

WRITE DOWN WHAT YOU LEARNT FROM THIS EXERCISE

HOW TO CREATE A POSITIVE MINDSET:

EXERCISE 2:

Make a list of all the words you tend to use most often in your vocabulary when talking with others.

Are they positive or negative?

Do these words evoke strength and success?

Do these words make you feel confident?

Do these words evoke weakness and failure?

How do these words make you feel now?

What kind of energy do you put into these words?

What kind of energy would you like to put into these words?

Does your language inspire others?

Reflect on various situations where you have used negative words. What positive words could you have replaced them with to make you and others feel more powerful?

Do you say the word, *but*, often? What if you replaced this word with the word, *and?* Would the outcome be the same?

Do you often say, "I can't?" What if you replaced those words with, "I can?" Would the outcome be the same?

Do you often say, "I try?" What if you replaced those words with, "I will," or, "I can?"

WRITE DOWN WHAT YOU LEARNT FROM THIS EXERCISE:

NOTES

NOTES

NOTES

NOTES

CHAPTER 2:

HOW TO STOP THE INNER CHATTER

*"It's not what you say out of your mouth that determines your life.
It's what you whisper to yourself that has the most power."*
– Robert Kiyosaki

It's that internal noise that goes on in your head, on a daily basis, that convinces you that you can't be/do/have something. It's the devil that sits on your shoulder every day, that whispers in your ear and tells you that you are not good enough, beautiful enough, or intelligent enough; that you shouldn't bother, you will fail, and no one loves you; that you are fat and ugly, and no one wants to be your friend, or invest in your business, or work with you. All these thoughts affect your mood; they make you unhappy, angry, restless, and anxious. They affect your ability to focus, and they interfere with your communication with others. These thoughts become monkeys in your head, screeching all day long, wanting to be heard and listened to. They sit on your shoulder like a devil. And guess what? We all have them.

They are based on belief systems that you have built up over a lifetime, based on how you have interpreted and emotionalised your experiences over time. Know they are all normal. Taming your monkey will give you clarity of mind, allowing you to focus on the present, increase your sense of calm and wellbeing, and make you feel happier. The challenge is how you deal with them.

STEPS TO STOP THE INNER CHATTER:

1. Accept that this inner chatter is normal; that you can tame that devil—that screeching monkey in your head.

2. Talk to that monkey, to that inner devil. Have a conversation with it. Stop and listen to what it is saying. What is it trying to tell you? Is it reality? Or just your imagination?

3. Make a list of all the inner chatter that is going on inside your monkey brain. Give yourself 15 minutes every day to write down what you are thinking and feeling, and about anything that is worrying you. Then stop. Tell your monkey mind that it's had enough of your time for today, and it can screech another day. Every time it kicks off again, keep saying, *"Stop,"* to yourself. *"That's enough for today. You can kick off again tomorrow."* Visualise yourself blocking that inner chatter with your hand.

4. Meditate – create space between you and your mind; control your thoughts. It will calm that devil on your shoulder, that screeching monkey in your head. It doesn't have to take a long time. Work with the time that suits you best. If in doubt, start with 5 to 10 minutes, or even less, and just build the time up slowly to a space that is comfortable for you, before you start to fidget, or become restless or distracted.

5. Interrupt your monkey mind with a mantra. Every time you feel it kicking in, repeat a mantra to yourself, silently or loudly. The more senses you can simulate, the easier it will be to distract that inner chatter. If you don't have a mantra, try this one: "I am enough. All works well for me, my children, and my family, in the most phenomenal, amazing way possible." Or, "I control the thoughts in my head, not you."

6. Try this great breathing technique to distract you. It can be done discreetly without anyone noticing. Breathe in deeply. Don't force it. Breathe in gently through your nose and out through your mouth to a count of 7. As you inhale, place all your attention on the crown of your head. Then, exhale gently, without pausing, and place all attention on your naval. Keep doing this a few times until you can feel and hear the rhythm of your breathing.

7. Engage in an activity. When your inner chatter is kicking off, distract yourself with an activity that will totally consume you: bake a cake, go for a drive, paint, write an email or a blog, go to the gym, call a friend ... do anything that will leave you with no room to be allowing that inner chatter to kick in.

Before you realise, you will be focusing on other things and will have forgotten to engage with the monkey. The noise will have disappeared.

HOW TO STOP THAT INNER CHATTER

EXERCISE 1:

This is a great exercise for when you are feeling anxious and have too much inner chatter going on in your life. I love it! You can do this exercise anywhere, whether you are sitting or standing, on the train, or walking down the high street.

Find a comfy place and close your eyes if you can; have your hands on your lap, and your feet on the ground. That's not always possible, so imagine you are sitting in a comfy place… I have done this exercise whilst walking the dog. Mentally scan your body from the top of your head down to the balls of your feet. Notice what you notice. Notice what you are feeling. Notice where that feeling is in your body, what shape that feeling is, the colour and density of that feeling, and the sounds associated to that feeling. If you were to touch that feeling, what would it feel like? How would that feeling vibrate throughout your whole body? What type of vibration would that feeling give out?

Be grateful for that feeling, and for the energy that comes with this feeling; and as you are feeling grateful for that feeling vibrating throughout your whole body, continue to say thank you. Work through the whole body, and when you have finished and are ready, open your eyes. This exercise will help you feel more relaxed, and will connect you to the *now* moment, into your own energy.

Use it, and practise it, every day. It only takes a couple of minutes. Whenever you catch yourself going into those negative feelings—that negative mind chatter that bothers you (e.g., feeling angry, sad, unloved)—STOP.

Remember, those feelings are not who you are; they do not define you. Those feelings are all about the energy you put into those feelings.

WRITE DOWN WHAT YOU HAVE LEARNT FROM THIS EXERCISE

HOW TO STOP THAT INNER CHATTER

EXERCISE 2:

This exercise is from Dr Frank Hladky, one of the greatest bioenergetics therapists of all times. It focuses on telling your mind to observe physical perceptions in your body; to notice the differences between one side of the body and the other; to notice the structure of your body, from the soles of your feet, to your eyes and face.

This exercise allows you to regain control of your mind, to raise awareness of your body, and to still the chattering monkey in a matter of a few minutes or seconds.

Start by looking at the soles of your feet. Is the left sole rougher than your right?

Look at your left hand. Does it have more veins than your right hand? Are your nails the same length on the left hand as they are on the right?

Is your left shoulder tighter than your right shoulder?

Does the left side of the neck feel more tense than the right side?

Does your right ankle have more moles than the left ankle?

Is your left eye the same colour as your right eye?

Is your left eyebrow the same shape as your right?

Does your left hand feel heavier than your right? Does it feel more tingly?

Does your left foot feel lighter than your right?

WRITE DOWN WHAT YOU LEARNT FROM THIS EXERCISE

NOTES

NOTES

NOTES

NOTES

CHAPTER 3:

HOW TO LOVE YOURSELF

"Measure your worth by the dedication to your path,
not by your successes or failures."
– Elizabeth Gilbert

Loving yourself is the art of self-acceptance: to love who you are unconditionally. It's the key to living a fulfilling and happy life. It means having a positive self-image and self-respect. None of us are perfect. We are all unique, a gift to this world. You have your own strengths and weaknesses, and in order to discover who you are, you have to invest further in your personal growth and development. Only you can do this, because until you see and love the light that shines within you, no one else will.

STEPS TO LOVE YOURSELF:

1. Stop comparing yourself with others. Just be yourself. Know that you are AMAZING. There is no one else like you. Never question this. Just accept it. Say to yourself, "I have everything I need within me to live the life I deserve. I am beautiful. I am unique. I am intelligent. I am worthy."

2. Learn to listen to your intuition: Too often, we try to be a people pleaser to everyone. Listen to your intuition, to what your body and mind tells you, and to the thoughts that hit you in the first 5

or 6 seconds. Do not listen to others. Be brave enough to know that you know the answer deep within you, and what is right for you, not for anyone else. I have learnt over the years that my initial intuition is always right, no matter what the outcome; and the moment I start to question decisions is the moment I lose control—the self-doubt kicks in.

3. Listen to your body: We are all on a treadmill, and pressures of daily life, coupled with social media, just make it worse. When you are hearing those early warning signs, you need to slow down, and breathe. STOP—listen to what your body is telling you. Take 5 minutes out. It's enough to put yourself back into control, back on track. Take a walk, do some breathing exercises, meditate, do yoga, blast out the music at home or in the car, treat yourself to a coffee, read a magazine. Sing, run a bath, ring a friend.

4. Make yourself a number 1 priority: So many of us put other people's needs first and forget to look after ourselves until the tank is drained or the cup is completely empty. Take time out every day to recharge, and don't feel guilty. Unless you have refilled your cup, you serve no one. You need to be mentally strong first, in order to be of value to others. So, pamper yourself with a facial, a massage, a meal out, cinema tickets, coffee in a café…. Just do it, one small step at a time, and not only will your confidence grow, you will also feel so much better.

5. Include fun in your life. Laughter is one of life's greatest gifts. When you laugh at yourself, you are practising self-love. Some individuals think they should only be focusing on goals—on serious stuff—and convince themselves that it's not important to have fun. However, laughter makes life more bearable. Spend time with your mates, relaxing with them and enjoying each other's company. Ensure that you see the funny side of life, and that you laugh at yourself and with others, and put time in your diary to *chillax* with those who count most.

6. Pay yourself amazing compliments daily. Make it meaningful. Put energy and passion into the words you use with yourself. Keep saying these to yourself, over and over again, until you really believe them. Keep writing them down. Put them on a note where you can see them around the house: in the office, in your purse, on the fridge, in a book, on your iPhone. Compliment others too. Write your bestie a postcard, listing her top 10 attributes, and carry out 3 acts of kindness a day. Help your neighbour with their shopping, or make a cuppa for your work colleague.

7. Stop blaming others for the pain that has happened in your past. It acts as a huge drain on your life. It is now time to release those negative emotions, to truly love yourself and to move on. Forgiveness is the gift you give to yourself, because you let go of all the blockages that are holding you back from shining your light. Journal these emotions, write them down on a piece of paper (even burn the paper like a ritual), meditate these thoughts, or speak these thoughts out aloud with a mantra: "I forgive myself for my actions. I forgive those who have hurt me, who have caused me pain. I set myself free."

HOW TO LOVE YOURSELF

EXERCISE 1:

Show daily gratitude for everything in life. It will shift you to a higher frequency, and you will attract better thoughts and opportunities into your life.

One of my favourite quotes: *"Your mantra is thank you. Just keep saying thank you. Don't explain. Don't complain. Just say thank you. Say thank you to Existence."* – Mooji

I always start and close the day with gratitude. I take 5 minutes each day, morning and night, to show thankfulness for all that is wonderful in my life, no matter how small.

I make myself a cuppa in the morning, go back to bed, open the window, let the fresh air breeze in (I love listening to birdsong), close my eyes, and start my gratitude. I say thank you for the day before, for my family, my friends—it can be for anything—for a friend calling me up to say hi, for a new client, a new invitation, for having healthy children, or for the birdsong I hear outside.

I do the same again before I go to bed, when my head is on the pillow; I say thank you for all that has happened to me during the day. There is always something to be grateful for, even if it is just to say thank you for having a job, a roof over your head, a pet, for being able to pay the bills, to have a family that loves you, friends, colleagues who support you … It makes you feel so thankful about your life, and is a beautiful way to fall asleep. It allows your mind to drift into a safe, relaxed space.

Do this every day. Put aside 5 minutes each day to say thank you for everything and everyone in your life. See how quickly the lens of your life changes.

WRITE DOWN WHAT YOU LEARNT FROM THIS EXERCISE

HOW TO LOVE YOURSELF

EXERCISE 2:
Have you heard of the mirror exercise? It is a great technique to help boost confidence, love yourself more, and believe in yourself and your potential.

It is best done in the morning, before you begin your daily routine, so that you start the day feeling energised and confident. Work out a time that suits you best in your daily schedule. It may suit you better to do this in the evening, or just whenever a handful of self-esteem is required. Do this once or twice a day, depending on how you feel, and make it a habit.

Stand in front of the mirror, with both legs slightly apart. Let the weight of your body be equally divided, and look at yourself in the mirror with confidence. Breathe in and then out. Compose yourself. Get yourself into the right mindset. You may feel uncomfortable or slightly silly doing this, but it's worth it. This exercise only needs 5 minutes. And as you become more comfortable doing this, you can talk to yourself for longer, or however long it takes for you to get that confidence boost, to feel good about yourself.

Now, smile slightly, and start talking to your reflection, aloud if possible. If others are in the house, and you can't do this, just say it in your mind.

Tell yourself positive statements: how amazing you are; how you can achieve anything; how your friends all love you; how you can do this; how you are unstoppable; how beautiful you are. Focus on one part of the body that you like best about yourself: Feet? Shoulders? Toes? Hands? Legs? Say to yourself, "I love my hair; it's curly, thick, and luscious. It suits my face really well, and it makes me feel sexy." Keep doing this, and you will see a difference in your self-esteem.

WRITE DOWN WHAT YOU LEARNT FROM THIS EXERCISE

NOTES

NOTES

NOTES

NOTES

CHAPTER 4:

HOW TO DEAL WITH OVERWHELM

"All great changes are preceded by chaos."
– Deepak Chopra

Overwhelm chaos occurs when you feel flooded with obligations and decisions. You feel you are being bombarded from all sides. You are unable to think clearly, can't cope with the inner chaos, and inner destruction has set in.

STEPS TO DEAL WITH OVERWHELM:

1. Understand why you are feeling overwhelm. Sit down quietly with a piece of paper and ask yourself: are you trying to do too much? To be everything to everyone at once? Is this serving you? Make a list of all the obstacles that are standing in your way. Organise the obstacles in order of priority. What's the largest single obstacle? If you could wave a magic wand and remove one obstacle, which one would it be? Which one obstacle, if removed, could help you the most to move forwards?

2. Admit you can't do it all. That's okay; it's normal!
   "It's better to do one thing right than ten things poorly."
   – Heather Hart.
   And allow yourself to say NO. You cannot do everything. Start being selective. Don't feel guilty, and stop worrying about what

others may say. They are not living your life. You are not a machine. You cannot be everything to everyone. Your cup needs to be full and not running on half or empty. When you take charge of your life, when you accept responsibility, you make giant leaps from childhood to adulthood. Your levels of confidence and courage start to exceed your levels of fear and doubt.

3.   Plan ahead. Start your day organised. Before you go to bed, think about your schedule for the next day—what goals you need to set—and then block your time out well during the day. Set deadlines and measures to each of these tasks. Do the hardest task first, as it will give you the most sense of achievement. Brian Tracy's, *"Eat that Frog*, is a fantastic read. He talks about personal time management, decision, discipline, and determination, and how you can waste your day focusing on the stuff that doesn't matter. So, do the scariest, hardest task first, at the beginning of the day. Don't wait till the end of the day, because the likelihood is that you won't do it, and it will roll onto the next day, and so on. Select one key goal to action. Remove all obstacles to achieve that goal. As Brian says, *"Without goals, you drift. With goals, you fly like an arrow—straight to your target."* So, fly straight to your target.

4.   In between your major projects, transition well. Give yourself time to reset, to find silence in between projects (e.g., delivering a presentation, taking calls, or responding to emails). Taking a mental break of 5–15 minutes will help you deal with the overwhelm. Take time out to meditate, go for a walk, have a cuppa, or sit quietly —whatever works for you in your schedule. Give yourself the gift of distraction. And stay off your mobile or laptop in this period.

5.   Give yourself the ability to catch up at the end of the day to ensure that tomorrow starts with a smile. Take 20–30 minutes at the end of each day to catch up—look at it as your safety time. If you can't

manage that time, take 10 minutes. Ask yourself: What do I need to catch up on today so all will flow smoother tomorrow and make me feel more in control? Do I need to reply to a few emails or make a couple of calls? Set a timer; then take the rest of the evening to switch off, to focus on yourself and your family.

6. Do a checklist: Are you eating enough? Eating healthily? Are you skipping meals? Having too much caffeine? Enough water? Exercising enough? Sleeping enough? Relaxing? Breathing in the fresh air? Is your mindset positive? Are you being reactionary or responsive at work and at home? Are you mostly happy? Sad? Irritated? All these factors have a huge impact on your mental and physical health.

7. Reward yourself: When you have overcome a challenge, treat yourself. Pat yourself on the back; buy yourself some flowers, or the book/dress that you have wanted for a while. Have some chocolate, a glass of wine...whatever makes you feel good—and say, "WELL DONE," to yourself. Tell your friends. Tell the world too. Let them enjoy and share your thunder.

HOW TO DEAL WITH OVERWHELM

EXERCISE 1:

(2 parts to this exercise)

1. Write down everything that keeps you awake at night, worries you during the day, and creates your inner chaos.

Do a brain dump on paper. Don't hold back; don't edit... just let your thoughts spill out, with no stopping. Ready, steady...Go!

2. Now you are going to put everything into an order of priority, and focus on what you can control rather than what's not in your control. For example, rather than worrying about you not getting clients, think about what you can do right now to attract more.

Take your list, and put a line through people, projects, etc.: people who you don't really want to spend time with; projects you don't want to be involved in; things you constantly feel guilty about; stuff that has been dragging on your to-do list for ages....

Be brutally honest with yourself. Get crossing.

Now you have a list of lines. See what's left, uncrossed.

It's time to refocus, prioritise, and get real stuff done, and if you haven't got enough lines, start all over from the beginning and repeat the exercise.

WRITE DOWN WHAT YOU LEARNT FROM THIS EXERCISE

HOW TO DEAL WITH OVERWHELM:

EXERCISE 2:

It is impossible to say *yes* to everything without there being an impact on you, your health, or your relationship with others. There are not enough hours in the day for you to be a superhero to everyone. You, saying *yes* when not really wanting to, is usually coming from a place of fear, or from a desire to help/please others.

Right now, you may be thinking, "But if I say *no*, my friend might not like me anymore." Or, "I won't get invited to another party," or, "I will hurt their feelings." The reality is, saying *no* can save your mental health, and if you continue saying *yes* to everything, you run the risk of burnout—of being so overwhelmed that your great intention leads to you becoming frustrated and stressed.

Let's work with an example of when you recently felt overwhelmed, and you said *yes* to helping someone when you really wanted to say *no*.

Did you allow other people's priorities to take first place over yours?

Did this impact your own wellbeing?

Did this impact your personal relaxation time?

Did it take you away from your family and friends?

Did it stop you from saying *yes* to the really important stuff?

Was it worth it?

WRITE DOWN WHAT YOU LEARNT FROM THIS EXERCISE

NOTES

NOTES

NOTES

NOTES

CHAPTER 5:

HOW TO DRESS WITH CONFIDENCE

"Self Confidence is the best outfit. Rock it. Own it. Wear it."
– Unknown

Your dress style is a statement about who you are. It's about an attitude, a way of life. How you share your personal story with the world. It takes confidence to put on a certain outfit, and this confidence, this energy, aligns with your whole being. It doesn't mean you have to buy an expensive suit or a sassy dress. It's about knowing what suits you—your complexion, skin colour, hair—what makes the best of your assets, and leaves you feeling good about yourself.

STEPS TO DRESS WITH CONFIDENCE:

1. Experiment with clothing. Find a style that suits you, your personality, and your lifestyle; one that makes you feel comfortable. Try new looks; look through magazines to see what you like; be ready to step out of your comfort zone. Go shopping with a friend to a department store—try on lots of different clothes; see which style works best for you—or ask an assistant for their advice. Above all, be open-minded. Until you try the garment, you won't know whether it suits you, or how it makes you feel. If not sure, take some photos on your phone, and show them to your friends. Let them help you find your new style. Ask them to be honest with their feedback.

2. Don't try and fit in with the crowd. Know your personal style. Own it, and do not be afraid of being different. That's your beauty. Think back to when you saw someone wearing something different—an outfit you secretly admired. You never had the guts to wear it, but you would have *sooo* loved to. What did you like about it? Could you wear it now? Maybe it is time to believe you can. Guess what? You CAN!

3. Shop with a colour palette in mind. Know the colours that suit you: the colours that make your eyes stand out, your hair dazzle, your figure shine. Understand how to wear colour correctly, to ensure that your look is flattering rather than a *sight for sore eyes*. Colour code your wardrobe accordingly so everything matches and makes it easier for you to choose your wardrobe.

4. Invest in a personal stylist and wardrobe consultant. Let them take the stress away from you. Connect with a consultant who understands your personality and lifestyle, and can work it into a wardrobe. And go with the flow. Let them work with you with new styles. Trust in the process, and just go with the flow. You might surprise yourself with the new looks they come up with—and find yourself a good hairdresser.

5. Never walk out the door feeling unsure about your outfit—if you are in a hurry and have no time to change, you will not like yourself all day. You will feel uncomfortable, and it will show to others in your body language. I always plan my outfit the night before, especially if I know that I am leaving the house early or catching a train. That way, I know that I will feel good in what I have chosen to wear all day, the moment I walk out my front door. If you are unsure about a piece of clothing, change it. Try something else until you find an outfit that works for you.

6. Consider your body shape. Knowing your shape is key to dressing with confidence. We are all different shapes and sizes; whether

you are apple or pear shaped, tall or short, there is always a great style that works well for you. Dressing for your shape makes all the difference; so, work with your beautiful curves to help you strut your stuff and own the look. It speaks volumes about you, about who you are.

7.   Consider the occasion. If you are a working adult, your wardrobe probably covers you for 3 different situations: work, social, and lazy home clothes. Being well-dressed starts with planning for the occasion. Look at your wardrobe, and ask yourself if you have the right wardrobe for the right occasion (e.g., for a job interview, office meeting, birthday party, black tie event, wedding, funeral). There is always a possibility that you will be pulled into an event last minute, so be prepared and never upstage the host or the bride/groom. Always check that your wardrobe is appropriate to any of these occasions.

8. Know your comfort level. Buy clothes and shoes that you are comfortable in and fit your body: shoes that won't give you blisters, and clothes that fit well, which aren't too tight or too big. If you can't enjoy how you look, all your hard work will be for nothing. It won't be appreciated by others. There is no point in wearing that bright red lipstick or that low cut top if you feel self-conscious. Start with small steps, build up your confidence slowly and, once ready, just GO for it.

HOW TO DRESS WITH CONFIDENCE

EXERCISE 1:

Take all the clothes and shoes out of your wardrobe.

Separate them into 4 piles:
- Ones you haven't worn for at least 2 years
- Ones that aren't comfortable
- Ones that you have never worn
- Ones you love

Next, throw all of these aside, apart from the ones you love.

Decide what you like about each piece.

Is it the colour?

The style?

The cut?

The texture?

How does this piece make you feel when you wear it?

When do you feel most comfortable wearing this?

Does it suit your shape?

Does it fit in with your lifestyle?

How could you further accessorize?

Make a list. This list can be the starting point for your next shop. You now have a better idea of what suits you.

WRITE DOWN WHAT YOU LEARNT FROM THIS EXERCISE

DRESSING WITH CONFIDENCE

EXERCISE 2:

Invite some friends round and do a catwalk at home. Tell everyone to bring their make-up and hair straighteners, and as many outfits and pairs of shoes they fancy.

Sell it to them as a great opportunity to work out outfits for different occasions: for the next office party, wedding, interview, date, night out. It's a time to giggle, laugh with your mates, and mix and match clothes. Get some nibbles in; maybe some wine too.... Play some funky music. Get the vibe going in the room.

You can decide to either stay in and get a take away or go out on the town after, once you are ready to strut your stuff.

Above all, have some fun with this. The purpose is for you to work out a style, or several styles that make you feel confident and good about yourself. It's an opportunity to ask your friends for their advice. What colours suit you best? What hairdo works well? How can you apply your make up differently? The more opinions, the better. Together, you can discuss and share ideas on how you can create the best look for yourself—to get that WOW factor when you walk into a room. And seeing a different look on your friends will give you new ideas too.

If someone has a mannequin, ask them to bring it along too—dress it up with your outfits. It can help you choose the right outfit, especially if you are a visual person. See how everything coordinates: whether it works well, and whether you like the final look. Include the shoes, jewellery, and handbag too. Work out a colour scheme for your make-up too.

WRITE DOWN WHAT YOU LEARNT FROM THIS EXERCISE

NOTES

NOTES

NOTES

NOTES

CHAPTER 6:

HOW TO STOP WORRYING

*"Worry does not empty tomorrow of its sorrow.
It empties today of its strength."*
– Corrie ten Boom

It is so easy for worrying to get out of control. One small thought can grow and escalate into something huge; so, unless you keep a lid on your thoughts, and control them, you can end up creating a mountain from a mole hill, feeling mentally and physically exhausted. Mental tension translates into physical tension. When you get that backache, headache, or stomach ache, it usually tends to be anxiety related.

STEPS TO STOP WORRYING:

1. Ask yourself if the problem is solvable or if it is out of your control. If it's solvable, sit down with a piece of paper and work out steps to chunk it down into small steps, with timelines, so it doesn't seem so overwhelming to you. If it's out of your control, let it go. There is nothing you can do to solve it, so worrying will not improve the situation. It will only create greater stress and anxiety within you and everyone around you. Take a deep breath and recognise this.

2. Create a worry period in your day. Choose a set time and place (make it early) so that you won't spend time in your day agonising

over whatever concerns you. Tackle it as soon as you can, give it your full attention, and then let it go. If need be, write your worry/worries inside a journal, shut the journal when your timed period is up, and do not open the book till the next day. If you need to reflect on what you have written, do this to distract yourself; and keep all thoughts in the positive.

3. Your thoughts and emotions are like leaves or feathers that fly past in the wind. They hit you like devils or monkeys; but know they are only passing thoughts that come into your life, pass through, and then fly out again. They are never here to stay. They do not own or define you.

4. Stay focused on the present. Pay attention to the way your body feels or reacts to a particular thought, and how your body rhythm changes when you find yourself stuck on a particular thought. Learn to become aware when you find yourself in this situation, rein your thought back in, and focus on the present. Meditation is a great way to calm down. It took me a long time to meditate (I am always running around; there's a reason why my nickname is Tigger), and it was only when I found the right meditation that the penny dropped as to how beneficial it was to me. There are great examples of meditation that you can listen to on YouTube. Download some peaceful music; find a calm, relaxing spot, and just begin. I even meditate on a train sometimes, to slow myself down by listening to my own breath. Five minutes can be enough to rebalance you.

5. Spend less time with people who make you feel anxious, who constantly make you worry, and fill you with their negativity. Think of friends and colleagues like a drawer of socks: You have socks with holes that you will never throw away; you have socks you have never worn and socks that you occasionally wear. The socks with the holes are the people that are important to you in life; the socks that you never wear are the people who have no meaning

in your life; and the socks you occasionally wear are the people that dip in and out of your life. Ask yourself the question: how many of those people make you feel good about yourself? Which ones would support you unconditionally? Which ones would say they support you but behind your back would be criticising you? Which ones would have the courage to tell you what they think? Which ones would say, "I don't understand. Help me to?" As my mum always says, "Choose your friends wisely. They will either build you or destroy you."

6. Get a pet. It's a fantastic way to relieve stress. The human-animal bond has shown that simply stroking or cuddling an animal can improve mental health, anxiety, depression, and loneliness in children, adults, and the elderly. Benefits are not just short term. Research has shown they help to lower blood pressure, slow heart rate down, and calm you.

7. Find a mantra that distracts you and calms you down when you find yourself in moments of anxiety. A mantra is a word, or a group of words, that is repeated over and over again to aid concentration in meditation, and you can utter these whenever you need to.

HOW TO STOP WORRYING

EXERCISE 1:

I love this exercise. It's simple and easy to use, and I have used it ever since my train crash. My wonderful boss, who helped me overcome my struggles during this difficult time, gave me such a gift with this strategy. I still use it to this day, 20 years on.

This technique helps me whenever I am feeling anxious: going into a new meeting, or a new situation, not knowing anyone and feeling slightly unsettled and nervous. It calms me down immediately. You can do it anywhere. Even in the loo.

Imagine you have a cloth roller blind above your head. Add a colour, a texture, and a width to it. Does it have a pattern? Or is it plain? Is it light or heavy?

Imagine the blind rolling down slowly: covering your whole body, starting from the crown of your head; rolling down slowly past your forehead, your eyes, nose, throat, neck, shoulders, chest, stomach, thighs, and ankles; right down to your toes and the soles of your feet.

As you imagine the blind rolling down, keep breathing in and out slowly; focus and listen to the sound of your breath. Feel the blind rolling slowly over your whole body.

By the time the roller blind has reached the ground, you should feel calmer and in control.

It might take a couple of times to get used to this exercise to start with, but keep at it.

WRITE DOWN WHAT YOU LEARNT FROM THIS EXERCISE

HOW TO STOP WORRYING

EXERCISE 2:

Another great exercise for stopping you worrying is known as the supermarket conveyor belt exercise. Imagine you have products whizzing by on a conveyor belt in front of you. Now, replace these products with your feelings and thoughts. Here's how it goes:

Set an alarm for 3 minutes.

Find a comfortable, quiet spot, and focus on a fixed point in the room. Close your eyes if you can, with feet firmly on the ground and hands on your lap.

Imagine your mind is like a conveyor belt.

Observe and describe everything (every single emotion and feeling) that passes by on the conveyor belt in front of you.

- What kind of emotions are you sensing?
- What kind of feelings are you experiencing?
- Do they have any connection to the present?
- Do they connect you to the future?
- Are these thoughts of any value?
- Do these thoughts serve you?
- Do they make you happy? Anxious or sad?
- Would you like to let them all go? Let them pass and blow away?
- What and who is stopping you from letting them go?

WRITE DOWN WHAT YOU LEARNT FROM THIS EXERCISE

NOTES

NOTES

NOTES

NOTES

CHAPTER 7:

HOW TO SELF CARE

"Sometimes the most important thing in a whole day is the rest we take between two deep breaths."
– Etty Hillesum

STEPS ON HOW TO SELF CARE:

Self-care is vital for your wellbeing. It's important to maintain a healthy relationship with yourself in order to stay confident, energetic, productive, and healthy in mind and body. Many of us have trouble in reading internal signals, so it's essential to remind yourself and others around you that your needs are important too.

1. Identify the activities that help you feel your best—ones that nourish you and make you feel good. Book a date in the diary, with yourself. Put time aside each week to read a book, learn something new, do a gym class, watch a film, write a journal, meditate, visit an art gallery.... Whatever the activity, make it fun. If possible, make time for yourself every day, even if just for 15 minutes; or, if easier, one hour a week. Pamper yourself with flowers, candles, weekend breaks, nights out with your mates, retreats... whatever rocks your boat. And enjoy the moment.

2. Self-care is about caring for your mental and physical health, eating healthily, sleeping enough, caring about your personal

hygiene, and exercising regularly. Think of your body as a temple. Your brain, like a car, needs quality fuel to drive it. How well do you look after your mental and physical health? Eating healthily and being active creates a more positive mindset and a greater self- belief, and confidence. How much time do you invest in this area? How well do you look after yourself? Scale yourself in each of these areas, from 1–10, with 10 being high and 1 being low.

3. Accept things as they are. Stop trying to push the river up the mountain. Accept that there are things in your life that you cannot change, and have no control over, so just go with the flow. Breathe and surrender. And I mean surrender. The hardest step is to let go for fear of the unknown. Sometimes it's just easier to trust that the current of life will take you in the direction you need to go, and that all will be well, and that all will evolve how it should. Why fight if you can step back? Enjoy, and live in the present.

4. Set time aside for daily reflection, at the beginning and end of each day. Focus on questions around your goals, behaviour, and general state of mind. Ask yourself these questions: Are you living up to your core values and personal mission? Are you living your life to your full potential? Are you giving your friends and family the most and best of you? Are you making a positive impact on this world? If you dropped dead right now, would you, by having been born, have made a difference to this world? If you could live your life again, would you live it any differently? Do you love who you are?

5. Stress Management is key to self-care. Whilst some stress is good for you, constant stress can have adverse effects on your physical and mental wellbeing. It's important to recognise stress in all areas of your life, as you need balance in order to live a healthy and deserving life. Ask yourself which areas of your life give you the most stress and why? What step could you take right now to reduce that stress? If that step seems too big, how could you

chunk it down? Who could help you? If you don't know how to do this on your own, sit down with a friend, someone you trust, and brainstorm. If all else fails, seek the advice of a mentor.

6. Keep a healthy work-life balance. It's easier to say than do sometimes. However, unless you find a way to strike that balance, you run a risk of burning out, and suffering from insomnia and exhaustion. Look at your home and work environment, and see how you can reduce stress in these areas. Take time out to have lunch. Don't eat lunch at your desk, and don't work till late. You are not being productive. Go out for half an hour, find a chill out space, and just be still. Absorb the sound of the wind, and the trees, the light, and the shadows, and the colours. Breathe and connect with yourself.

7. Stop comparing yourself to others. It only leads to unhappiness, envy, and inadequacy, and a drop in your confidence. Ask yourself how it makes you feel when you do this. Focus on your strengths rather than on your weaknesses. Be aware of when you start comparing yourself to others; when you recognise the signs, block those thoughts. Focus your energy on what's great about you, on what you have, and not on what you don't have. Appreciate who you are, the things you love, the wonderful friends and colleagues who exist in your life, and the blessings that life has given you.

HOW TO SELF CARE

EXERCISE 1:

The wheel of life is a fantastic self-assessment tool for personal development, to create balance, happiness, and success in your life. It originates from Tibetan Buddhism and focuses on 8 components, which are also called happiness factors in human life.

It represents 8 sections, which together, represent one way of describing your life. Balance is required in all areas in order to find ultimate happiness in your life. Reflect on the balance you have in each of these. Draw a wheel. Break it down into 8 sections. Add the categories below.

Rate your satisfaction in each area, from 1–10 (1 being the lowest and 10 being the highest). This scoring will highlight the life satisfaction of each of these areas.

Decide which area you would like to improve. Ask yourself what score you would like to achieve in a specific time (set a date). What would be the ideal score for you? How could you achieve it? How would you know you had achieved it? Draw a wheel, and let's start.

- Career
- Health and wellbeing
- Finances
- Family and friends
- Romance
- Personal development
- Fun and recreation
- Physical Environment

WRITE DOWN WHAT YOU LEARNT FROM THIS EXERCISE

HOW TO SELF CARE:

EXERCISE 2:

We are all leading busy lives, and research has shown that even minimal exercise is better than nothing. It can impact on your overall health and wellbeing, both physically and mentally; so even just walking the steps in the tube, rather than taking the escalator, can get the heart rate pumping. Small steps create action.

Any form of exercise increases endorphins to the brain. The benefits are endless. Exercise helps you to think more clearly, increases your energy and productivity levels, impacts on stress and depression, speeds up your metabolism, and makes you feel good about yourself. It's proven that it takes 21 days-plus to change an activity into a routine, and once you get the mindset fixed, you can start upping the exercise and making it more intensive.

Here's a list of a few things you could try:

Look at your daily exercise routine. How often/much do you walk in a week, or do you travel everywhere by car?

What are your favourite forms of exercise? What's open to you where you live? What exercise classes/groups can you join? Running Groups? Walking Groups? Yoga/Pilates/Keep Fit classes? Cycling? Swimming?

Get off one stop earlier on the tube or bus.

Check out and download online fitness apps, on your smartphone, to get healthy and stay fit. Invest in a pedometer.

Take your dog for a longer walk; add 5 minutes onto your routine.

Check out your diet; how healthily do you eat?

WRITE DOWN WHAT YOU LEARNT FROM THIS EXERCISE

NOTES

NOTES

NOTES

NOTES

<h1 style="text-align:center">CHAPTER 8:</h1>

<h1 style="text-align:center">HOW TO REFRAME A NEGATIVE THOUGHT
INTO A POSITIVE ONE</h1>

*"Once you replace negative thoughts with positive ones,
you'll start having positive results."*
– Willie Nelson

STEPS ON HOW TO REFRAME A NEGATIVE THOUGHT INTO A POSITIVE:

1. Write down all your negative thoughts. Find evidence for and against each thought. Question the validity of each thought. Which ones are a figment of your imagination? Which ones have substance to them? Be honest with yourself. Then, negate each thought with a positive sentence. Even if you don't believe what you write down, write it down (e.g., No one wants to be my friend = Everyone loves me; or, I am not intelligent = I have wisdom in areas others do not.).

2. Brainstorm: The purpose of this exercise is to instil hope and open your mind to new opportunities and possibilities. If your biggest problem is currently your finances, write down whatever springs to mind that could resolve this situation (e.g., you getting a better job or part time work, cutting back on expenses, getting a promotion, winning the lottery). Have fun with this. Draw a *spider-o-gram,* with lines going outwards (as many as you can, to offer

you solutions that you may not have thought of). Let your imagination roam free. I always suggest doing this out of your home environment so that you don't get distracted. A café is always a great place, or just somewhere quiet where you can think.

3. Visualisation: I practise this daily, putting images and descriptive language to my thoughts. I visualise the outcome I would like to receive from anything that is happening in my life. I visualised me becoming a radio presenter. I visualised every single detail—who I wanted to work with, the show I wanted to present, the people I wanted to interview, what I would wear, who I would interview— and guess what? It became a reality. You can do the same for any goal you have in mind.

4. Daily Reflection, day and night: When you go to bed, or when you get up, replay any negative outcomes that are playing on your mind, and reframe them to a positive outcome. What could you have done to make this outcome better? (Even if you do not believe this, the subconscious will reset itself.) I do this every day. When I wake up and sit in bed with a cuppa, I set my mindset for the day. I think about the outcome I would like to achieve for something, and if I am feeling anxious about anything, I reframe it into a positive. Life is all about challenges. They hit you unexpectedly, so practising this technique helps you deal with these moments. Mel Robbins', *The 5 Second Rule,* is a fabulous tool. She talks about how each thought stays positive for only 5 seconds before the inner chatter kicks in.

5. Practise positive thinking and a positive attitude, and expect success. Take control of your life. You are the boss of your life. Always focus on the positive. So, when it's raining, don't think about your hair getting wet, and that you are going to get drenched. Think about how fabulously your garden is getting watered. The more you practise this, the easier it will become. Set

a timer in your phone to remind yourself, at least twice a day, to reframe your thoughts (at least 5) into positive ones. And remember: any thought that pops into your head is either a flower or a weed—you decide; you control it.

6. Schedule time in your diary for positive activities, for your personal development. Listen to your favourite song. (Mine is, "Proud," by Heather Small. It makes me reflect on my life purpose.) Listen to podcasts or YouTube, or read a book. Life is all about learning, and the more you learn and listen, the more wisdom you will gain. I love YouTube and audible books; so, when I am walking the dog, I tend to listen to an audible. Sometimes, too, when I am walking down the high street and want a few moments to myself without being stopped by friends, I put my headphones on, not to listen to anything but to give me time out to reflect.

7. Reframe disappointments, challenges, and failures into moments of huge growth and learning. Again, these are all moments of huge reflection, part of our daily ups and downs. I reframed my moment of surviving a train crash, into a moment of huge learning. I talk about this in the book, *The Pay it Forward Series: Notes to My Younger Self*. Eighteen coauthors from around the world talk about moments of adversity in their lives, and I chose to share mine in order to give others the courage and the strength to share theirs, to know that all and everything is possible. That train crash gave me my life purpose—to become a mentor, a confidence generator, a public speaker—to motivate you to use your voice, to Dream, Think, and Play Big.

HOW TO REFRAME A NEGATIVE THOUGHT INTO A POSITIVE ONE

EXERCISE 1:

Start by paying attention to your thinking. Catch yourself every time you have a negative thought, and write it down. You will be amazed by how many pop into your head.

Keep a diary for a week.

Work out where they occur.

When do they occur?

At what point of the day?

How many times a day?

Which people set them off?

How do you block these thoughts?

Do you block them?

Can you block them?

How do they make you feel?

How could you reframe them into positive thoughts?

WRITE DOWN WHAT YOU LEARNT FROM THIS EXERCISE

HOW TO REFRAME A NEGATIVE THOUGHT INTO A POSITIVE ONE

EXERCISE 2:

You have the choice to decide whether every thought you think is positive or negative.

Imagine every thought that pops into your mind, either as a seed or a weed. You can either water the seed with positive thoughts so that the seed flourishes into a beautiful flower, or you can throw negative, destructive thoughts at it until it wilts and eventually dies. The choice is yours. You hold the power in your hands.

Take 5 negative thoughts that you have regularly, and reframe them into positive thoughts.

Here are some examples:

I am not good enough = I am awesome.

I am sick and tired of getting things wrong = I am getting better and better every day.

I can't do this = It might be difficult for me at first, but when I achieve this, I will feel amazing.

No one likes me = Everyone loves me.

Why do I keep making mistakes = How lucky am I? I am learning new things every day.

I just don't like him = None of us are perfect. Everyone has their strengths.

WRITE DOWN WHAT YOU LEARNT FROM THIS EXERCISE

NOTES

NOTES

NOTES

NOTES

CHAPTER 9:

HOW TO DEAL WITH CHANGE

"The greatest discovery of all time is that a person can change his future by merely changing his attitude."
– Oprah Winfrey

Everyone is afraid of change. For some, it can be very unsettling, and even frightening. Change hits us when we least expect it. The only difference between you and the other successful people you admire is how you move through it in order to get to where you want to be. We are never prepared for change, and we never know how we will react to this moment; whether we will be reactive or responsive. Our response to change is one of these three, or maybe all three: fight (taking the challenge head on), flight (running away), or freeze (rabbit in headlights, not knowing where to turn or what to do).

STEPS TO DEAL WITH CHANGE:

1. Change your response. Your attitude will determine how you deal with change. So, accept the fact that it has happened. Acknowledge it will happen, whether you like it or not, and think how you can best deal with it. Change the mindset, the beliefs you hold around your fear. Your beliefs change constantly as you experience new challenges, travel, and meeting new people.

2. Face your fears. List all your fears, and give them a score of 1–10, depending on the level of fear they represent. Then, score them again on how inconvenient the fear is for you. Choose the first 3 you think are the most inconvenient to you, and tackle those first. Ask yourself the question: "Am I going to tackle my fear of...?" Chunk your fear into small, manageable pieces, and add a timeline to each of them so that you can easily deal with each one at your own pace.

    So, for example, if you know you are about to be made redundant, don't ignore the situation, thinking it might not happen to you. Work out a plan B, find the right people to advise you within the company, and then take action.

3. Communicate your feelings. It's key to how you work through this period of transition. Share how you feel with someone you can trust. Do not be afraid of exposing your vulnerability. The moment you surrender and express your fears is the moment you move from fear to love. And don't feel you have to wear a mask for the outside world. Just be you, your real self. Others will respect you for it, and you will inspire them with your strength and courage.

4. Remember, there is always a positive in every challenge, in every moment of change. It's important to remember this when you are frightened and confused. Scheduling physical activities into your diary can help: a brisk walk, a dog walk with a friend, or a gym class can help. Look at your daily routine, and work out what you could do to refocus this state of mind. Make a list. Take time out for yourself, and sit in the garden, with no phone—just yourself— and think about all the positive learnings you are experiencing in this moment. Listen to the birdsong; look at the leaves on the trees, and the colour and texture of the flowers in the garden. Notice what you notice.

5. Visualisation or mental imagery is a simple act of quieting your mind, and can help you deal with change. This simple tool inspires

you to take action, to visualise whatever you want without limitations, and to reframe your picture. As we visualise, we can see ourselves having and doing all the things we want. We begin to become more confident in ourselves, and the more confident we become, the more action we take. I tend to do my visualisation when I am in bed, before I nod off to sleep. I visualise something I want to achieve; I rerun it in my mind, like a film, over and over again, adding colour, feelings, and texture to all the images, being as creative in the detail as I can.

6. Be flexible and embracing of the change; stop trying to control your emotions. Rather, focus on taking your emotion in the direction you would like it to go. Accept, too, that sometimes all is out of your control, so you may just have to go with the flow: lean into the fear; don't fight it; take one small step at a time; find your courage (you will inspire others through it); and enjoy the ride. It's going to be a great one!

7. Stop the fearful thoughts. Fear is an illusion. It is not real. It is made up of the stories we tell ourselves, embellished to major heights through our imagination, until we are completely petrified. Change the stories you tell yourself. Learn to live in the safety of the present moment. Mantras always work for me. Every time I am feeling fear or anxiety, I repeat a mantra to myself. Here are a few you might like to try. Dr Google is great for finding out more. There is a list at the end of this book too.

"I CAN," or, "YOU CAN DO THIS."

HOW TO DEAL WITH CHANGE

EXERCISE 1:

Choose a time in your life when you were faced with huge adversity, or when you think that you failed or let others down.

Write down all the feelings and thoughts associated with this time.

How did this event impact you, your family, and everyone around you?

How did you respond to this situation? Were you responsive or reactive?

Did you bury your head in the sand, hoping the situation would go away?

Did you run away and not deal with it?

Did you face the challenge head on?

Or was it a combination of all 3?

Had you reacted differently, would the outcome have been the same?

What did you learn from this challenge?

How did it make you step out of your comfort zone?

What positives could you take away from this?

Now, moving forward, focus solely on the positive lessons learnt. Let them become your strengths.

WRITE DOWN WHAT YOU LEARNT FROM THIS EXERCISE

HOW TO DEAL WITH CHANGE:

EXERCISE 2:

We all love familiarity. It makes us feel comfortable and safe. However, it can also stop us from living new adventures and experiences. Why is it that we tend to take the same route home, or choose the same dishes in a restaurant, or wear the same style? Simply put, we wish to stay in our comfort zone and not be challenged with possible change.

Here is a really simple exercise to see how you respond to change:

At your next work or social meet up, rather than choosing to sit in the same seat or next to the same person, choose to sit next to someone you have never spoken to before, in a different spot in the room.

Or, why not approach someone in the room you have never spoken to before, and simply introduce yourself. Walk straight up to them and start a conversation.

What is your initial response to this?

How does the thought of doing this make you feel?

Does it fill you with excitement or dread?

You prepared to do this. Why? If not, why not?

What if you do this, and it's not as difficult as you thought?

What's stopping you from doing this?

What is the most challenging part of this exercise for you?

WRITE DOWN WHAT YOU LEARNT FROM THIS EXERCISE

NOTES

NOTES

NOTES

NOTES

CHAPTER 10:

HOW TO COMMUNICATE POSITIVELY

"The single biggest problem in communication is the illusion that it has taken place."
– George Bernard Shaw

It's essential to talk and to communicate well with others. Keeping your emotions bottled up can lead to stress, misunderstanding, illness, and anxiety. Speaking to mentors, friends, colleagues, or strangers can help you reflect on what's going on in your life, to help you gain a different perspective, and advice and support. Just talking through something out loud can help you to see a situation very differently, to see light rather than darkness. As my gran always said, "A problem shared is a problem halved." It takes courage to share problems with others; but once you start, you will notice the difference it makes: it helps you to feel less alone, more supported, and understood.

STEPS TO COMMUNICATE POSTIVELY:

1. Check your body language. We all have the intention to communicate well. We all communicate in different ways, but we don't always communicate in the best way. Our body language may convey another message to others. Pointing a finger at someone, using foul language, putting hands on hips, or shouting, doesn't say much about you. It just shows that you are out of control and letting yourself down. So, if you feel that moment of

anger coming on, step away until you have calmed down and are ready to communicate positively. Remember, it's not what you say; it's how you make someone feel that counts.

2. Use the 48-hour or number 5 countdown rule. If someone has upset you, or something is making you feel angry, rather than firing off on all cylinders, remove yourself from the situation, and give yourself time to think (48 hours). Always reflect before you open your mouth and blurt out whatever it is you want to say. Life is not always black and white. There's grey—loads of different shades of grey in between—so don't look for a fight. Try to see the other person's point of view too. Neither one of you is right or wrong. You just have 2 different perspectives. You can also count from 5 backwards, until the moment has passed when you wanted to say something. So, loads of deep breaths first...

3. Find the right time to have a conversation about something that is troubling you. Don't engage in a conversation if someone is rushing out the door to catch a train, or is about to go into a meeting or make a call. Choose your moments carefully, when you are both relaxed and can spend time together to talk it through. If need be, schedule in a time. Think also about the type of language you will use with the other person—one which will work best for the both of you to receive the best outcome.

4. Repair disagreements. Apologise when you have hurt or upset someone with your words or actions. Appreciate that they may be more sensitive to you. Your language may have been confrontational, and it may have affected them more than you think. Talk it through with them rather than letting it fester away inside of you. Find a common ground for the both of you to move on from. If there is no common ground, accept the relationship for what it is, and move on. Hugs, laughter, kisses, cards, and flowers always help to improve communication, and are always gratefully received.

5. Value other people's opinions. Everyone has the right to be heard and to have a voice. You might not always like or agree with what someone is saying. It doesn't mean you have to ignore what they say or dismiss their feelings. Think how you would feel if no one listened to you or felt you had anything of value to say. Every time someone expresses an opinion, it takes courage. So, be kind, and listen to what they have to say; and respect them for their opinion. You would want the same respect.

6. Be confident in your ideas. If you are entering a new situation, and you know that certain topics will be discussed that you have no clue about, do some research. Understand the topic so that you can contribute with more confidence rather than worry that you will have nothing to say.

7. Accept feedback as being constructive. It is never a personal attack. So, whenever you feel that someone has criticised you, don't feel defensive; take a step back and put the emotions aside. Reflect on the conversation to understand whether there is true value in its meaning. Become an observer, and ask yourself if there is any truth to contribute.

HOW TO COMMUNICATE POSITIVELY

EXERCISE 1:

Think back to a recent moment in your life when you struggled with your communication, when you needed to have THAT difficult conversation.

- How did you communicate nonverbally?
- How did you communicate verbally?
- Do you express yourself clearly?
- Did you make assumptions during that conversation? Were they correct?
- Did you pick up on what was *not* being said?
* Did you listen to them, or just to your own voice?
- Did you use the other person's communication style and body language?
- Did you get the right response?
- How could you have handled it differently?
- How could the conversation have changed if you had altered your communication style and body language?
- How did it make you feel?
- How did it make them feel?
- Are you happy with how you managed this conversation?
- Was it a win-win situation for all?

WRITE DOWN WHAT YOU LEARNT FROM THIS EXERCISE

HOW TO COMMUNICATE POSITIVELY

EXERCISE 2:

Listening is key to communicating effectively and, as we all know, 5 people can have the same conversation, and each can interpret it very differently. Usually, 60% of people remember the first word; 75% remember the last word of your conversation; and 20% will remember the obvious word you never said.

This is a great party or team game. You can also make it fun. One person whispers one fact to another individual. They pass it on to the next, and so on.

As soon as you have passed the message on, write down exactly what you shared.

The last person who hears the message, shares it out loud with the group.

Each of you then shares the message you passed on, with the person sitting next to you.

Is the initial message identical to the last one shared?

How has it changed in the sequence? Why has it changed?

Discuss why it can sometimes be difficult to *hear* what is being said/relayed in a conversation. What can impact your listening skills?

Reflect on whether you really listen to others: All the time? Some of the time?

Do you always give someone your full attention? How do you give them your full attention?

WRITE DOWN WHAT YOU LEARNT FROM THIS EXERCISE

NOTES

NOTES

NOTES

NOTES

QUOTES TO INSPIRE YOU

(Here are a few that I created myself. You can do the same.)

"A shift of your mind can change your whole life."

"Let's do this."

"Life is short. Stay awake for it."

"Be the person you want to meet."

"I believe I can, and I so will."

"Confidence and lack of confidence are both infectious."

"I will hate myself if I quit just because it got hard."

"After the rain, there is always sunshine."

"Worrying changes nothing."

"I am strapped in, ready for take-off."

"Life is bitter or sweet, like a recipe. And that's what makes it delicious."

"Life is not perfect. Be happy with what you have. It's beautiful."

"People may want you to fail, but I have found a way to be strong, and so can you."

"My expectations stop me from achieving my goals."

"If I don't try, I will never know."

"I can change my hair, my clothes, my makeup, but unless I change what's on the inside, I haven't changed a thing."

"Why be a shadow of the woman you want to be. Find your voice from within."

"You have to create your own sunshine because no one will reach up to the sky and do it for you."

"There is a rainbow in every cloud. Even if you can't see it, it is coming. Enjoy the ride."

"I was born to make a difference, not just to make a living."

"There is beauty in every struggle; that is, if you choose to see it."

"Don't ever let anyone destroy your dream."

"To change your life, you have to change the way you think and feel."

"My name is irrelevant. What matters is the footprint I leave behind."

"My words are an asset, not a liability."

"Talk is cheap without action."

"We are going to be alright."

"Every thought I think, every word I speak, is creating my future life."

"Real achievement requires unstoppable action, and unstoppable action requires passion. You will never achieve anything by simply thinking about it."

MY QUOTES ... time for me to create some quotes that will motivate me to live my dream, to be confident, respect myself, and love and honour the wonderful, beautiful person I am today.

ABOUT THE AUTHOR

"Life for me is all about confidence. You are not born with it; you are taught it. I truly believe that each and every one of you has the power within you to maximise your full potential, with the right tools, influences, and positive mindset. Challenges hit you every day; that's part of the journey—to grow and be taken onto your next stage of creativity, development, and inspiration. Your actions will, in turn, inspire others and future generations to believe in themselves. Give yourself permission to Dream Big—to know that you have the desires and all the tools within yourself to create the life you deserve. Never give up on your dreams. Change the stories you tell yourself, and change the beliefs you surround these stories with. You are the master of your own ship, so take the wheel, and start living the life you deserve. The only person who holds you back is yourself. This book gives you the tools to grow in confidence, spread your wings, and fly, to become the person you dream to be."

Ania Jeffries is a global, award-winning coach; a number 1, international, best-selling coauthor of the book, *Pay it Forward: Notes to My Younger Self;* a mentor for The Princes Trust; founder of Women Work; a radio broadcaster and features presenter for UK Health Radio.

TESTIMONIALS

Amazingly insightful...this book is deserving of the tag MUST READ.
Stewart St Clair
TheWayForward Show at UKHealth Radio

Ania Jeffries is on a mission. A woman driven by her desire and passion to make the world a better place for the next generation. Everything she does is focused around empowering others to be the change and lead the change. Through her public speaking, event management coaching and radio broadcasting she has has provided women of all ages with a platform to find their voice, speak their truth and follow their hearts, so it comes as no surprise she has written a book about increasing confidence. This book is jammed packed with the words of wisdom she wishes to share, as well as the tips and tools she has picked up along the way. Through writing this book, she has allowed the next generation to step forward with confidence to put their best foot forward and to follow their dreams no matter where it takes them.
Kezia Luckett
CEO and Trailblazer behind the Women of Contribution Movement

Ania Jeffries is an incredibly energetic and compassionate Confidence Generator. Her skill set is not just about helping others to find their WHY. She specialises in personal development, confidence, empowerment and self improvement. She is totally dedicated to giving others a voice worldwide, empowering others to identify the right relationships in business and personal growth, to build strong global collaborations and networks.
Mike Rebello
Chief Influencer, Epirrion

Ania has found one of the keys to becoming the person you really should be: Confidence. With it, the world can once again be your oyster. And with this book you can boost your confidence in 24 hours. From the very first chapter you'll have practical advice, that once applied, will restore your uniqueness, unleash your inner beauty and give you the tools to take on anything and become the person you should be. And if you are generally positive about life, this book will help you stream positivity in everything you do and into everyone around you. I'm confident that Ania's book will work wonders for you. It did for me.

Barnaby Wynter
PLC Communications Director and Brand Speaker